VISIONS

Susan Joy
Menchell

Text copyright © 2019 Susan Joy Menchell
Front cover artwork by Susan Joy Menchell

Inside book illustrations © 2019 Aphrodite Mirisis Edited by Aphrodite Mirisis

These are original works of poetry. All rights reserved.

Library of Congress Control Number:2019916222

ISBN 978-0-578-59044-8

First Edition: 1995

DEDICATION

For my grandmother, Rose, in whom I felt full trust in another's love and who taught me the value of hard work.

For Linda, who has taught me many things, and continues to show me the value of patience and the meaning of true friendship.

Lastly I dedicate this book to my mother, Doris Menchell, and my sister, Faith Pollack, for encouraging me to pursue my painting and writing throughout the years.

Contents

PART I STRUGGLES	1
Love Escapes Me…	2
Now	3
Remaining	4
Daddy	6
Light	8
Unloved Woman	9
I Emerge	10
Rain	11
About Honesty	12
The Tiger	13
Autumn	14
Untitled	16
The Black Narcissus	17
You	18
In Simple Terms	20
I Fell in Love With the Blues	22

PART II INSPIRATIONS | **23**

Everything, Anything, and Nothing	24
Iron Worker	25
Under the Bridge	26
Sand and Sea	27
Grandma's Violets	28
Hospital Home Care	29
For Ira (A brother lost)	30
For Lucy	32
My Mother	33
Elegy for Essie	34
Billie	35

PART III CHANGE AND GROWTH 37

Idols Fall	38
Flow	39
To Cecil	40
Fear of Heights	41
A Place	42
Broken Eagle	43
Metamorphosis	44
You Never Put Your Heart on the Line	45
The Cat's Back	46
Freedom's Gate	47
Solitude, Acceptance, and Love	48
Feeling Fully	50
Children Again	51

Part IV LOVE & SELF ESTEEM   **53**

Combined Minds	54
No One Dares	55
The Sound of the Heart	56
Gold	57
Finding Love	58
Wings	60
Going Within	61
Fling (Lyrics to a Country Tune)	62
I Miss You	63
Sometimes (Lyrics to Another Country Tune)	64
Never	65
The Wind	66

PART I
STRUGGLES

Love Escapes Me. . .

Love escapes me,

I have no clue

Of where to find it-

It's as elusive

As a beautiful dry red leaf

Blown in the wind;

When I try to grasp it,

It crumbles

At my touch

Now

Now-
Now I remember her
Brushing my hair
And telling me
It's just like "woven gold"

Now---
Now I remember the pain
Of the nightmares
And her comforting me
Just sitting next to me

Now----
Now I remember the fear
Of losing her love
And never wanting
To make her angry

Now----
Now I hold the child
I once was –in my heart
As it leaves my soul
To never return again

Remaining

Kill the illusion
And find the real man
That's what I'll do
No voodoo
No witchcraft
No daily horoscope
Will do
It's no longer true
That any of you
Men
Can save me
From myself
With reality
Coming in
Steadily
I'm bound
To change
So will you
And the Illusion

Of two as one
Will change too
And that's OK
Cause I'll remain
    Me
And you'll remain you
And maybe we'll
    Grow
And maybe we'll
    Learn
But we'll no longer
Send smoke signals
From fires we burn
Because it won't
    Be needed
When illusion dies
    Real words
With real heart
Can only remain

Daddy

God died the day you were born
Daddy
No one knew; not even you
What a trail of sorrow
Can follow a man's misgivings
There was always a fear of you

Even when you cuddled me
Next to you at 4 or 5
On Sunday mornings
In you and Mom's big bed
I remember apprehension

The hate came much later
Maybe at 10 or 12
I don't know
But it's stayed with me since then
Like a grey cloud
Following me into
Every new relationship

One quick gesture
Of a man
Can send me cowering
Or ready to strike
The slightest disagreement
Becomes a full scale war

What did you do Daddy
What did you do
That makes my soul stay bruised
As the skin of that 10 or 12 year old

People say—don't hang on to those memories
But how do I let go
When horror looms
Over my new dreams

Light

The light bursts through the haze
And the mystery no longer exists
Clearly there are reasons

For all
      our
          behaviors

The shame is that
Sometimes we go backwards
To whom we thought we were
And then we learn
We are different
And can no longer remain
In our old shedded skin

Those who have insight
Will see us for who we are
And also who we are becoming-
And accept us

In the light,
We are no longer obligated
To explain ourselves
To those who can't fathom change

We must keep to our course
And try to remain
Consistent with the light
Of our inner self
That's constantly being formed
As we live

Unloved Woman

        I am a cauldron

        Of heat and flame

        Self- consuming,

        In disarray-

        I am the soul

        Of an unloved woman

I Emerge

There's a child at play

That was never there before

There's a lady who sings

Now present in my soul

There are wings

Of a bird in flight

No longer haughty

But with grace and agility

As the wind

Slowly becomes my friend

And a long standing absence

Of heartfelt solitude

Suddenly gladdens me

As never before

I emerge whole

Rain

Rain falls

Like tears

In a soul

Lost to

Grief

And

Apprehension

Rain falls

Like the

Torrent

Of emotions

I

Can't

Hold in

Anymore

About Honesty

Do you ever come by
Just to come in
Not to borrow or take

Do you ever need shelter
I know this need I can't fake

Why then don't we enter
Saying "I need to feel secure,
I need to feel whole, I need to talk"?

And talk with meanings
Not more lines from a Hemingway plot
Where the people don't mean as much
As the bullfight behind

Let's put ourselves in each others' places
Saying what we really mean
God, how full of life
Your being with me might be

Don't you see
We talk to impress
We talk at; over each other

Why is it, two human beings
With different lives
Can't be honest
If that's all there is to talk about –
Just being honest about themselves

The Tiger

The Cat Lies Sleeping
While the Tiger is at play

Everyone Senses It
No one knows the way
To become
A BIGGER ANIMAL
Have a fuller SELF
than the child
we were given.

F O L L O W   the tiger
dancing and bouncing.
Through the steps to to full adulthood
Watch her GROWL, and watch her CLAW
SEE the truth
About her
S L O W L Y
Come to be KNOWN

Autumn

The sky is a blend of light and small streaks of
sunny day clouds
And the birds sing of a peace only nature's doing
I sit, wind blowing through my hair
Attentive to the season's changing
Wrapped in flannel
Waiting for my own internal changes
To stay with me and become me-
As the leaves become the trees in Autumn:
The red, yellow, green settles
my longing
And the sky whispers
"in due time, in due time"

I come forth on the path of the unknown
Surely shaken if not disheartened
For change is a leaving behind of old
Yes we must forget in order to grow
And the ducks fly in their forever "V" formation
Amazing me each time they come and go-
Can nature carry me within its plan,
Out of the plan I've recently smashed:
Realizing it was only a false ideal-
Can nature bring me to my senses;
I'll try to stop the day-in-day-out repetitions
And instead I'll make it my own life
So that freedom will remain in my own hands

Untitled

Like a shadow I trace the lines of the missing face I had
Longed for
Like a dream I see myself wanting to follow you through
Crowds just to watch
Do you remain forever childlike, does the man ever
emerge
How can I tell, unfortunately I can't

A whisper of sound comes through my lips when I speak
of you
Now
The tenacity of my longing is dying down as the flames
flicker
In the wind
Self- knowledge brings me a new longing to separate
from all
Who seek to control me
I become a shadow of the child you once called your
lover

Dreams of a higher order replace the fantasies of youth
Streamlined relationships beckon me to their calling

Games I once was thrilled by have become an annoyance
I am growing towards taking my life seriously

The guilt I once felt in wanting the love of a man now is
A dream of mine
The fear of others not understanding my depth no longer
is angering me
I'm loosening the constrictions youth had placed on me
I am and will always be the way nature intended me---free

The Black Narcissus

You go on alone
So you'll go unquestioned
Leaving all virtues you had
In their hands- as if they
Are the only ones who see you

You go on alone
Valuing only time
Without others who are
Possibly wiser without us
To show you a path

You are the Black Narcissus
You are the dying embers
Of an almost whole man
You are giving nothing

You "contain" harm you say
You can't control life
Without keeping others away
But why, why feed on pain

You are the darkened angel
Who cannot find his way
You taunt me
In your overt
Confused state-

You

You stalk me
Like a cat
Springing onto
Its prey

Will you eat me
Forgetting
Why you
Launched
Paper boats
And bottles
With messages
To me.

Will you forget
I'm human
And want to hunt me
To prove
Your power
Your strength –

Can the games
Be halted
for civilized
Debate and
Conversation.

It's not clear
Why you fear
Exposure

I'm not sure
Privacy, dear –
Is that dear

I watch
While you
Sharpen
Your teeth

Against the
Stone
Wall
Of boredom

And you
Ready
Yourself
To
Gobble
Me down

Thinking
I'm a "Sitting Duck"

But you're
So wrong
And being
So right

Is something
I must
Get used to.

It's not clear
Yet it's clearer
Why
You fear
Exposure.

In Simple Terms

We all live in the same world
Yet try to avoid each other's glances
As if we were hiding a truth-
That might somehow connect us

The separateness we cause ourselves
Is the result of our pride
Forgetting we can share our burdens
Of life with each other

We are so many beads,
Intertwined on the same necklace,
Yet we refuse to touch

We attempt to break loose
But we can never do so,
And will be forced
At some point
To look at the small space
We occupy,
 In the continuous strand

No longer alone
No longer separate
We may always be superficially different
Yet in life-
We can never be so distinct
So that there is no connection possible
We rebel, and fight and taunt mostly ourselves
In trying to remain
Completely separate from others-

On the other hand
When we join in the dance
And can look clearly at those around us
Without hatred or fear-
Then we are truly free

I Fell in Love With the Blues

The water has lost its gleam
No matter rivers, streams or ocean
My devotion to missing you
Remains and stays

And all I hear is the Blues
How could I have loved and finally lost
How could I be the lonely downhearted
one

I don't know anymore
What became of the thrill
Of living, since I lost you
Not only did I lose you
But I lost your love, your heart

And nothing is here
To replace the emptiness without you
I surely know a lovers' lament
And fell in love with the Blues

PART II

INSPIRATIONS

Everything, Anything, and Nothing

You can have
Everything
Anything
And
Nothing
All at the
Same time

You can think
Of having everything
Not choose anything
And therefore
Have nothing

Iron Worker

It's not in the impression left
After the slow hard crawl up in the iron

It's in the mind
Of the man who knows
What all men and women are capable of

It's not in the proof of ability
Or the undeniable repetitions
Of great feats

It's the ability of one's own will
To guide someone
Where they know they're able
And willingly want to go:

This is where the magic is

Under the Bridge

Under the bridge
Lights yellow and green
Mix with the waves
Moving, flickering

Under the bridge
I sat pondering
How strange
The old tires, broken bottles
The algaed rocks
The cars and trucks above
And the water
All meet

No black and white here
All substances
Blend together here
No way for me
To concentrate on one form
Without taking in the others

Under the bridge
A resolution of sorts
Overcomes me

I feel no need to hurry
I feel no need to connect
I am another substance
Blending, yet separate
Separate yet certainly not alone

Sand and Sea

The storm calms
So the seas
Can roll over the sand
Without crashing

The sea can
Turn stone to sand
With time
So that sea and sand
Will mingle as if one

The sun warms the shore
So that by day
It is walked past
And made love to

Yet at night
Mystery pervades all
And the sea and sands
Mingle slowly and part alone at times

The black night
Leaves only sound
For one's soul to contemplate
To some it represents freedom
To others, loneliness
These are the choices of our solitude

Grandma's Violets

Violets all in a row
I planted her violets
It was the Spring before I left home
I got down
On my hands and knees
In front of mom's house
And picked and pulled
Until the monument was finished

Who knew it was Grandma's own heart
The love she'd given me
That made me plant these violets
One by one, slowly and carefully
As my love for her had been gained
As my loss needed to be exclaimed
Who would've known, only she

Hospital Home Care

I feel like John Q. Public
Hands on my knees
Leaning and listening

Hearing you from miles away
My face blank, expressionless
Not like yours –
Filled with good sentiment
Truly worried about the System;

Good Hospital Home care
We need Good Hospital Home Care

Money is allocated
Money here, money there
Budgets, people's personal problems
All this at 8:00 a.m.

A window blows in
Sunny April air
And I suck it in

And I feel like John Q. Public
Hands on my knees
Leaning and listening
My face blank expressionless

For Ira (A brother lost)

Nobody will ever love me
Like Ira did
A hand to hold
A secret to tell

A heart lies broken
Bleeding, always bleeding
For the man
I never came to know

And I shed a tear
For Ira;
Yet no one saw
No one ever knew

How hearts in desperation
Can place hurt and lies
Into a separate place
While love grows

And while his body grows old
And numb –
In a place
Too cold for me to ever go . . .

I hold a place inside
For all his soul
Ever needs to be free
For I was his and he mine
And no one can steal
His memory from me

And I shed a tear
For years of need
When he was gone
And I'd searched for this feeling

Remembering when a simple 'hello"
Made my soul shine
And he'd sit with me
To let me know his world

And I took in only
A short span of time –
That I now look at
As if it were gold

And I thank Ira
For giving me a vision
And a longing to be free
Just as he had wanted for us
A long time ago

For Lucy

When it's so quiet
I wonder what she thinks of
When it's so still
I wonder how her heart doesn't break

Can we all be so strong
Can we all be so steadfast

Death is inevitable
And yet she smiles
She laughs at herself
Can't see, can't hear

But she remembers
Yet sings to me every rhyme
That she remembers

And as long as she remembers
No, not what she ate today
But the smiles and songs
And mostly the laughs of yesterday

As long as she remembers the good
Dying is the smallest part
Of all that she's lived

My Mother

The cold cold place
She sends me to
Hurts
Especially when it's your mother
Who sends you there

She doesn't know
Or has long forgotten
What love is
Or how she appears

My mother tries to feed my heart
With gold and gifts
She has tasted love
So long ago she's forgotten it –

My mother has regressed
To the days of her past
And she knows her lie:
Is that she just doesn't care

She becomes a carefree child
Whenever the mood takes her there
Where there's no longer a reason
For her to try to be
The woman her mother
Told her to be

My mother is sad, so sad
That tears come to me
Each time I look in her face

Elegy for Essie

Close your eyes
Now you're at rest
Peaceful and calm
That's all you asked for

Your heart
Too open for this world
Burst, split in half
Over the illusions
And the realities of life

I loved you
The best I knew
But healing broken hearts
Is simply not simple

So close your eyes
And forget all
Except the love
You did receive
For the love you gave
Goodbye forever
Essie

Billie

Billie could sing it
And sway her voice
To the sound of the beat
With complete abandon

The way we are
When we allow ourselves
Full freedom to feel and hurt
And live fully

Billie could sing it
The way I live it
And I can tell
The difference
Between her voice
And the imitators

No one else
Could hold on
To the song
The way we hold memories
The way her notes live on in me

PART III

CHANGE AND GROWTH

Idols Fall

Idols
Fall
Better
Beings
Than
Me
They
NEVER
Were

Idols
Fall
Where
Tears
Used
To

And I knew you
All this time
Yet I feared I'd
Find
IT
OUT

Flow

Rivers roll and streams flow
Yet sometimes we won't go along
We get tangled in the old rubbage
We won't leave behind
Forgetting the ease of the ride
When we just let go

Rivers roll and streams flow
But the human mind
Gets caught in the mazes of negativity
And in blazes of torment
That trail behind us
Like a shadow

Can kindness be beckoned
Can that cat of our minds
Lay to rest
The fury of our unresolved souls?
There's nowhere else to go
But inside ourselves,
 We must flow with the tides

To Cecil

May all of your dreams come true
Though you don't want me with you
I'm not sure who did what to whom
Who first decided to part
But we both have a broken heart
Who thought love cost so much
And took so much work
To keep it flowing on
The river that is life
Is as dark as it is deep
And so easily drowns us in it
Without many bridges built
To cross over the emotional seas
What happened to you and me
I thought we were building our own bridge
        Together
As it turned out we went
        Separate ways
I wanted something solid
And you wanted something else
Something spectacular
Some bridge that joins all others
And covers miraculous lengths

Fear of Heights

Standing on the roof
I see nothing but train tracks
And trees and an old house

On the roof
Across from me
A bird trills in time
To some instinctual rite

Must be
A long lost friend
From another life-

And I'm thrilled
At his compliments
To my whistling

A train passed
Without a change
In the atmosphere-

And for some time now
I haven't told you
But I've been losing
My fear of heights

A Place

I'll find a place to fly
A place made for me

I'll find a place to land
A place between who I've been
And where I'll be

And while I'm there
I'll revel in that place

I'll find that place
Where you stand still
While you're still moving

Like time can feel
When it's passing quickly
Like a bird gliding

Broken Eagle

Broken eagle
Flies
Tempest torn

Split
Between
Pride and glory

Broken eagle
Needs the determination
To break through steel

Though barriers
Are grand
In size

She can fly
Way high
Above it all

And the walls
They'll fall
All for the envy of her

Metamorphosis

In the ocean of your eyes
There were no buoys or lines
And I, swimmer of all seas
Rough, deep, shallow and calm
I dove straight into you
Like the mermaids of old-
I felt no restraint in love,
I came apart, though
In the wanting of more and more
And nothing could fulfill me
Aside from a chemical cure
I knew that was not right
As I struggled from sea to land
In order to spread my wings
And ready myself for the future
    Flight
But with so much hesitancy
That you faltered at the
    Sight
Of my new wings
As did I, but we know
Nature draws me to flight-

You Never Put Your Heart on the Line

You never put your heart on the line,
You're always saying you're trying
to find
Yourself
You don't open up
anymore than a clam
And too many times I felt the slam
Of anger
There's a saying that must pertain
But why Lord can't I think of it now?

I'm only saying how hard I was trying
To get a message across to you
While you left me sitting
alone
Constantly singing and playing the blues-
If my guitar has a heart
It's heart is broken too-
You never put your heart on the line
You're always afraid of playing the fool.

The Cat's Back

The cat's back;
The distant feeling
Of someone there
Of someone watching

The cat's back;
The slow movements
Of someone thought out
Of someone clever

Nothing you can pinpoint
Nothing very noticeable

The cat's back, though
And I thought I'd lost
And no one believes differently
And no one wants to either

Slowly my feelings resort
Slowly
Reasons solidify

And somewhere within
As long as I believe
No one else must know
That the cat's back

Freedom's Gate

My passions run unbridled
Never claimed, never sought
Like a stallion runs wild
Never tamed by respectable men

My fears are few
Yet pain stops me-
Not the physical;
The deeper pain
Of lost time
And of lost dreams

I am no man's property
I've never been this
And will choose never to be
Considered anyone's property

There's a high price, though
That I pay
To continue my stance
Towards freedom's gate

Solitude, Acceptance, and Love

Rise, rise out from the internal pain
By giving to another
Giving your love
Giving your acceptance

Try, not for anything aside of humanness
To draw on
To be at peace
To be freed of misery

Love yourself
And of all the trials
You will have known
You will not lose this one

Love yourself
And in selfishness
You will no longer
Find satisfaction

The burden of loneliness
Is willed on those who cannot see
Outside themselves
Who cannot feel for another

The burden of sorrow
Is willed on those
Who sink into themselves
To avoid knowing
Who they are

Solitude
Is a wonder

When cherished

It is becoming
As many jewels
May be worn to adorn us

Solitude
Can be a jewel
Worn within us

Acceptance
Is a peace unsurpassable
And unattainable to most

It's a feeling
That must be worked for
And like many dollars
Will be spent and saved
and re-earned,
With each new parting
and commitment
Love is an endpoint
of all that we can learn
Words are too finite
To describe the capabilities of love

Once we can accept ourselves
And find peace in our solitude
We can allow others
Their space and freedom

We may give them our feelings
While accepting their feelings
At the same time

Feeling Fully

The calm returns
Like a welcome friend
And I open a door
That I had shut long ago

I see the shadows
Drift by me
But the fears
Cannot stop the longing

Freedom
This is my goal
And I know
This is my final destination

I gave my heart
So apprehensively
That I failed
To express all I felt

But now
I am starting anew
Relieved of old obsessions
And of old guilt

Children Again

Can we be children again
So that we don't forget
How to pretend
So that we don't forget
How to fully feel

Can we be children again
So that we don't forget
How to laugh
So that we don't forget
How to love

Can we be children again
So that we live for
Each day each minute

Can we be children again
In our adult lives
So we don't forget
All the important things-

Can we be children always
So we never stop
Yes- so we never stop growing

Part IV

LOVE & SELF ESTEEM

Combined Minds

I've combined minds
And so therefore-
Trial and error
Becomes my way to learn
It's a delicate thing
That we know of a soul,
It's a delicate balance
That we know life itself
We'd dance on barbed wire
Some of us surely would
If we thought it comfortable
In our tormented hearts-
I've combined minds, though
That of the daredevil and the dove
Where this places me
I don't even know yet
But love takes me there
And that is the reason
I'd have done anything I know-
To have gotten that love
Now I know the way
That is simplest;
Simply by caring
And by not hiding

No One Dares

      No one
          Dares
          Question
          Me
          Becoming
          Rooted
      Entangled legs
      And warm
          Kisses
      We both breathe
           Together
      Feeling
          The
      Present
      As much
      As any time
      That's passed
      Before us;
      As ever
      Important
      As ever
      Knowledgeable
      Of
      Freedom
      As ever
      Able
      To choose
      Choices
      We never
      Had
        Seen
         Before
         Either
           Of Us

The Sound of the Heart

Listen
Listen gently
To the sound

Listen
Listen with all your might
With all your soul

For hearts unchanged
Can never know
What lies within

Come along with me
On a path that's new

Listen
Listen sweetly
To the sound
What we wish for
Can be found

In the sleepless nights
In our longtime yearnings
In the quiet mornings

Together, alone however we come
On a journey to meet ourselves

Listen
Listen gently
Hear the sound
The sound of the heart
Beating like an eternal drum

Gold

Gold is a color
We may or may not see inside ourselves
We contain
What it is we want to contain

We bring ourselves
To our destiny
By believing in
What we already carry inside ourselves

Gold is not
The color of jewels
Or money or booty

Gold is the color
Of dreams
We allow ourselves
Because inside we are good
And feel worthy
Holding all the power to be whole Trustworthy and loved

Gold is
The color of love
Pure and bright
Unwavering, enlightening

Gold is
The color of truth
Of motivation

Gold is light
Clarity
The essence of purposefulness

Gold is the power
To trust yourself

Finding Love

    Love is not
-     clinging to another
-     to free you

    from loneliness

    Love is not
-     burdening yourself
-     to free another

    from pain

Love is not free
Love is not worthless
Love is not abundant
Love is not sex

Love is not a decision you make

Love is not
- a thing
- a substance
- or a thought

Love is a feeling of connecting with another
Love is spacious, allowing you room to grow

Love is non judgmental,
Letting you be genuine
Love is difficult to find
And very valuable

Love when omitted
- can stop a child's appetite
- or break a man's spirit
When given freely
Can change our fate
And bring us to sanity

Denied or given
Love changes us all

Wings

I must build my own separate identity
My larger self
True of heart and of mind
With no conflicted goals

There is a Pegasus
In my soul
A weighty persona
Yet with wings
Magnificent wings
Strong and healthy

I will be self- reliant
My own best friend
A free spirit
With dreams anew
No longer
Weighted
With self- doubt

Going Within

I close my heart to you
For right now
As you've done to me

You're so much like I was
You've had
No mirror
For too long a time

You're gasping
For breaths of strength
That you carry (of course)
Within yourself

No one ever told you
So you've never dared to look

Fling (Lyrics to a Country Tune)

I want some quick satisfaction
Not a very long- term thing
Just some a kissin' and huggin'
One of those old fashioned flings

Some people say you're too old
Some people say it's no good
All I know is when you hold me
It feels just like it should

I say come on over
You say you can't wait
We don't bother with formalities
We never needed to have a date

I'm just fine with a lover
We don't know if it'll last
Every time we get together
We always have a blast

So, baby come on over
You don't have to wait
Dress any way you want to
Don't let it get too late

I want some quick satisfaction
Not a very long- term thing
Just some kissin' and huggin'
One of those old fashioned flings

I Miss You

I miss you-
Neck kissing neck,
Fantasies of never
      Ever leaving the bed
Was it so simple or was it too difficult
      To ever do again

I miss you but not the loneliness
You inspire by not giving your all
Tongue in my mouth
I see other virtues now
In remaining chaste

You melted like the snow
Maybe I will remain changed now
Reflecting on the impermanent nature
Of all life brings with it
I miss some part of myself you inspired
Which has since vanished with the rains
Arms holding each others' waists
Touching skin not revealed to others

I want the grace of others unknowing of
Our time together
I want the time to remain forever with us
Like stone, like wind, like sand-
No longer transient but valuable

Sometimes (Lyrics to Another Country Tune)

I saw him last night with someone that I know
When I asked him what was goin' on he said
We're sorta dating but tonight we came alone
So he danced a dance with me as she watched
But, I had to ask him again- then he said

Sometimes we come together and sometimes we
    Come apart
And I looked in his big brown eyes and laughed
And said – I know what you mean, I know what
    You mean

Not too many men ask me to dance, because
Well, I know the steps and if I don't I
    Improvise
And girls can dance and sing and it don't
    Mean
They're fallin' for anyone in particular
But to the boys if they hold ya
They really wanna know ya

Like he said- sometimes we come together,
And sometimes we come apart
And me I'm keepin' a hold on my heart
Cause I know what it means, I know what it
    Means

Never

I've never loved and lost
Because I've never loved fully

I've never loved and known
A man's whole heart to be mine

I might have touched on the idea of love
Or the illusions of love

Somewhere, sometime
Love will come to be mine

Somewhere, sometime
I'll find
A love that frees me

There's a power to it
I'm sure I've felt
In her presence

The Wind

The wind circled
And then turned away

The wind of change
Never stayed by me
Only passed and waved

It took long hours
Pondering questions and longings-
        To see
That in order to change
One must reach up

Reaching high enough
To grasp the wind
With both hands and finally fly free

Hope you enjoyed this book. There are more books to come.

SJM

www.ingramcontent.com/pod-product-compliance
Lightning Source LLC
Chambersburg PA
CBHW071413290426
44108CB00014B/1801